food
glorious
food

fuel *britannia!*

The UK and Ireland are home to a glorious selection of delicious dishes – from hearty meals like cottage pie, roast beef and Irish stew to proper puddings like trifle, crumble and fruit fool. And in this mouth-watering new cookbook, you'll find Free and low-Syn versions of all your favourites. They deliver 100% on taste while helping you keep your weight loss on track – proving that a Brit of what you fancy really does do you good!

In fact, our islands' best-loved recipes are ideal when you're Food Optimising because so many are packed with fantastic Free Food. Made using lean meat from our pastures, fish from our seas and fresh fruit and veg from our fields and gardens, they're guaranteed to fill you up and keep you feeling full.

Our *national treasures* are the recipes loved in every corner of the land (and which appear on any self-respecting pub menu!), including fish & chips, bangers & mash and five classic roasts for the weekends. Our *local heroes* are dishes forever linked with a particular place, like Lancashire hotpot and haggis – and if you haven't tasted regional treats like Dublin coddle or cawl before, we think you'll soon be converted!

Our islands' best-loved recipes are ideal when you're Food Optimising

Essential vegetable dishes like roast potatoes and minted mushy peas are all here too, and we've saved the best till last. Sweet sensations such as orange & strawberry trifle, rice pudding and lemon meringue pie are the crowning glories of any meal – and our low-Syn versions are more tempting than ever before!

contents

Tuck into the hearty
dishes loved by one and
all, from cottage pie
and the full breakfast to
irresistible roast beef or
tender leg of lamb.

Bring some local colour
to your table with our
selection of regional
favourites, including
scouse, Dublin coddle
and Glamorgan sausages.

...and two veg

Make your meal into a masterpiece with our selection of essential side dishes, such as roast potatoes, minted mushy peas and colcannon.

happy ever afters

It doesn't matter how fu you are – there's always room for a pudding! Choose from traditional treats like rice pudding and gooseberry fool.

national
treasures

We may not always have the best weather in the UK and Ireland but our fabulous food always puts big smiles on our faces! In this chapter we slash the Syns of the classic meals and roasts loved in every corner of our beautiful islands.

honey-mustard roast beef
with roasted roots

serves 4

1½ Syns per serving

❄

ready in 1 hour 15 minutes

---

topside joint of beef, about 1.2kg, visible fat removed

1 tbsp mustard powder

1 level tbsp runny honey

salt and freshly ground black pepper

a few sprigs of fresh thyme, to garnish

300ml boiling beef stock

1 level tbsp gravy granules

for the roasted roots

1 swede, peeled and cut into thick batons

1 celeriac, peeled and cut into thick batons

3 carrots, peeled and cut into thick batons

2 tsp dried thyme

low calorie cooking spray

The more-ish honey-mustard mixture takes beef to a new level in this succulent Sunday lunch – and the filling roasted roots make a tasty change from potatoes.

Preheat your oven to 220°C/Fan 200°C/Gas 7.

Put the beef in a large non-stick roasting tin. Mix the mustard with the honey and 2 tablespoons of water and stir until nice and smooth. Spread the mixture over the beef and season generously. Roast for 20 minutes, then reduce the oven temperature to 190°C/Fan 170°C/Gas 5 and roast for a further 30 minutes for rare, 45 minutes for medium and 1 hour for well done.

Meanwhile, cook the root vegetables in lightly salted boiling water for 10 minutes, then drain and spread them out in a large non-stick roasting tin. Season, sprinkle with dried thyme, spray with low calorie cooking spray and roast for about 20-25 minutes, putting them in the oven about 10 minutes before the beef is cooked so that they are ready at the same time.

Remove the beef from the oven, scatter over the thyme sprigs and cover with foil to keep it warm. Leave to rest for 10-15 minutes.

Meanwhile, make the gravy. Bring the stock to the boil in a small pan and add the gravy granules. Whisk and cook for 3-4 minutes until thickened.

Carve the beef into thin slices, and serve with the roasted roots and gravy.

beef wellingtons

serves 4

6 Syns per serving

ready in 40 minutes,
plus soaking, cooling
and resting

15g dried porcini mushrooms

low calorie cooking spray

2 shallots, finely chopped

1 garlic clove, finely chopped

200g chestnut mushrooms,
finely chopped

small bunch of finely
chopped fresh parsley

salt and freshly ground
black pepper

4 large filo pastry sheets

4 beef fillet steaks,
visible fat removed

If you have a special occasion to celebrate, this fabulous dish of tender beef fillet wrapped in crisp filo pastry is the perfect meal to serve – and it will save you more than 10 Syns on the standard versions. Some say it was named after the Duke of Wellington, the British general who defeated Napoleon at Waterloo.

Put the porcini mushrooms in a bowl, cover with boiling water and soak for 20 minutes. Drain, saving the liquid, and finely chop.

Preheat your oven to 220°C/Fan 200°C/Gas 7 and line a baking tray with non-stick baking parchment.

Place a non-stick frying pan over a medium heat and spray with low calorie cooking spray. Add the shallots, garlic and the porcini and chestnut mushrooms and fry for 3 minutes, stirring. Pour over the reserved mushroom liquid and cook for a further 3 minutes or until all the liquid has evaporated. Stir in the parsley and season, then transfer to a bowl and leave to cool for 20 minutes.

Cut a pastry sheet in half and lay one piece across the other to make a cross or star shape (depending on the shape of your sheets). Place one of the beef fillets in the middle and spoon over a quarter of the mushroom mixture. Bring up the sides of the pastry to encase it tightly, scrunch it up at the top and spray with a little more low calorie cooking spray. Repeat to make the other wellingtons and spread them apart on the baking tray.

Bake the wellingtons to your liking (10 minutes for rare, 15 minutes for medium-rare or 20 for well done). Leave to rest for 5 minutes before serving with roast potatoes and your favourite vegetables.

cottage pie

serves 4

Free

❄ (without the egg)

ready in 1 hour

1kg potatoes, peeled and chopped

salt and freshly ground black pepper

low calorie cooking spray

1 red onion, finely chopped

2 garlic cloves, crushed

2 celery sticks, finely chopped

2 carrots, peeled and finely chopped

500g lean beef mince (5% fat or less)

400g can chopped tomatoes

1 tbsp vegetable stock

1 tsp sweetener

2 tsp dried oregano

1 egg, lightly beaten

The humble cottage pie has been a dinner-time favourite for more than 200 years and no wonder – it's still the simplest way to turn beef mince, fresh veg and mashed potatoes into something special… and completely Free!

Cook the potatoes in a saucepan of lightly salted boiling water for 12-15 minutes or until tender. Drain, return to the pan and mash until smooth. Season well and set aside.

Meanwhile, spray a large non-stick frying pan with low calorie cooking spray and place over a high heat. Add the onion, garlic, celery and carrots and stir-fry for 5 minutes. Add the mince and stir-fry for 5 minutes, then add the tomatoes, stock, sweetener and oregano and stir well. Bring to the boil then turn the heat to low and simmer for 12-15 minutes.

Preheat the oven to 200°C/Fan 180°C/Gas 6.

Transfer the beef mixture to a casserole dish and spread the mashed potatoes over the top, smoothing the surface with a fork (adding a pattern if you like). Brush with the beaten egg and bake for 25-30 minutes or until lightly golden and bubbling. Serve with your favourite vegetables.

To make Cumberland pie, whizz 40g wholemeal bread in a food processor and scatter over the pie before baking along with 25g grated reduced fat Cheddar (the breadcrumbs and cheese add 2 Syns per serving). For shepherd's pie, use lamb mince but remember to count the Syns (lamb mince with 20% fat is 4½ Syns per 100g).

steak
and kidney pies

Few meals sum up our islands quite like a hot pie!
Our low-Syn version is filled with satisfying chunks of
tender beef, kidney and veg in a sensational savoury
sauce, topped off with irresistible crispy pastry.

serves 4

4½ Syns per serving

❄

ready in 45 minutes

Preheat your oven to 220°C/Fan 200°C/Gas 7.

Spray a large non-stick frying pan with low calorie cooking spray and place
over a high heat. Add the steak, kidneys, carrot, celery, mushrooms, onion,
Worcestershire sauce, garlic salt, thyme, stock and gravy granules and stir
well. Bring to the boil and cook, stirring occasionally, for 6-8 minutes or until
thickened. Spoon the mixture into four individual pie dishes.

Cut the pastry into four equal pieces. Put one piece of pastry on a sheet of
non-stick baking parchment and roll into a shape big enough to cover one of
the pie dishes. Brush the rim of one dish with a little egg, add the pastry lid
and seal the edges with a fork. Make a hole in the top of the pie and brush the
lid with a little more egg. Repeat to cover the other three pies then bake for
15-20 minutes or until the pastry is golden.

Serve hot with wholegrain mustard (½ Syn per level teaspoon), and your
favourite potatoes and vegetables.

*If you don't have individual pie dishes you can use one
large baking dish instead.*

low calorie cooking spray

300g lean beef steak,
visible fat removed,
cut into bite-sized pieces

100g lambs' kidneys,
white cores removed,
roughly chopped

1 carrot, peeled and diced

1 celery stick, diced

200g baby button
mushrooms, halved or
quartered if large

1 onion, finely chopped

2 tbsp Worcestershire sauce

1 tsp garlic salt

1 tsp finely chopped
fresh thyme

300ml boiling beef stock

1 level tsp gravy granules

100g light puff pastry

1 egg, lightly beaten

beef stew
with dumplings

serves 4

4½ Syns per serving

❄

ready in 2 hours 45 minutes

---

low calorie cooking spray

700g lean beef steak, visible fat removed, cut into bite-sized pieces

2 garlic cloves, crushed

2 onions, roughly chopped

4 carrots, peeled and cut into chunks

2 turnips or 1 swede, peeled and cut into chunks

600ml boiling beef stock

2 tsp dried mixed herbs

salt and freshly ground black pepper

for the dumplings

50g plain flour

25g vegetable suet

small handful of finely chopped fresh parsley

For the ultimate comfort food on a cold night, you can't beat a good stew – and our light dumplings steal the show!

Preheat the oven to 160°C/Fan 140°C/Gas 3.

Spray a large non-stick casserole pan with low calorie cooking spray and place over a medium heat. Add the beef and stir-fry until browned. Add the garlic, onions, carrots, turnips or swede, stock and dried herbs. Season well, cover tightly and cook in the oven for 2 hours.

Meanwhile, put the flour, suet and parsley in a bowl. Add a pinch of salt and 2-3 tablespoons of cold water and mix well to make a soft dough. Season well and divide the dough into eight equal pieces. Shape each one into a ball and set aside.

Lift the lid of the casserole and place the dumplings on top of the stew. Cook uncovered for a further 20-25 minutes.

Spoon the stew and dumplings into warmed shallow bowls and serve with your favourite vegetables.

leg of lamb
with garlic and rosemary

Nothing says springtime like roast lamb, and a little rosemary and garlic makes the flavour unforgettable.

serves 4

Free

❄

ready in 1 hour 30 minutes, plus resting

1kg leg of lamb, visible fat removed

8 garlic cloves, sliced

12 rosemary sprigs

salt and freshly ground black pepper

Preheat the oven to 190°C/Fan 170°C/Gas 5.

Put the lamb into a non-stick roasting tin. Pierce the lamb all over with a short, sharp knife and push in the garlic and rosemary sprigs. Season well.

Roast the lamb until cooked to your liking (about 1 hour 20 minutes for medium or 1 hour 40 minutes for well done). Cover with foil and rest the meat for 10-15 minutes before carving into thin slices.

Roast lamb is sensational served with roast potatoes and your favourite vegetables.

Mint sauce is the classic partner for roast lamb and the no-added-sugar variety is Free. Even better, make your own Free mint sauce: finely chop the leaves of a large bunch of mint then stir in 6 tablespoons of boiling water and 2-3 tablespoons of wine vinegar (white or red). Add a little sweetener to taste.

roast pork
with apple sauce

serves 4

1½ Syns per serving

ready in 1 hour 30 minutes,
plus resting

1.5kg pork loin joint,
visible fat removed

salt and freshly ground
black pepper

1 tbsp passata

2 tbsp white wine vinegar

2 tbsp mustard powder

small handful of
finely chopped fresh
rosemary leaves

for the apple sauce

2 apples, peeled,
cored and chopped

1 tbsp finely grated
unwaxed lemon zest

1 tsp sweetener

This classic partnership brings together two of the things the UK and Ireland do so well: perfect, juicy pork and crisp, sweet apples from our beautiful orchards.

Preheat the oven to 220°C/Fan 200°C/Gas 7.

Put the pork in a large non-stick roasting tin and season well.

In a small bowl, mix the passata, vinegar and mustard powder. Spread the mixture over the pork and sprinkle with the rosemary.

Cover the roasting tin with foil and roast for 1 hour 20 minutes, turning the heat down to 180°C/Fan 160°C/Gas 4 after 30 minutes. Remove the foil for the last 15-20 minutes of the cooking time to give the meat time to brown. Remove the pork from the tin, cover with foil and rest for 10-15 minutes. Drain the cooking juices from the tin into a cup or bowl, spooning off and discarding any fat from the surface.

While the pork is cooking, make the apple sauce. Put the apples, lemon zest and sweetener in a heavy saucepan with 3 tablespoons of water. Cover and cook gently for 15-20 minutes or until the apples are soft and mushy. (This sauce can be served hot or at room temperature.)

Carve the pork and divide between plates. Pour over the reserved cooking juices and serve with the apple sauce and your favourite potatoes and vegetables.

gammon
and egg

serves 4

Free

ready in 10 minutes

4 large lean gammon steaks,
visible fat removed

freshly ground black pepper

1 tbsp mustard powder

low calorie cooking spray

4 eggs

Gammon steaks have a fantastic flavour and a little mustard makes them even tastier. Serve with chunky chips for a meal the whole family will love.

Preheat your grill to medium-hot.

Season the gammon with black pepper and the mustard powder. Grill for 4-5 minutes on each side or until cooked through.

Meanwhile, spray a non-stick frying pan with low calorie cooking spray and fry the eggs until they're done to your liking.

Divide the gammon steaks between plates, top with the eggs and grind over a little more black pepper. Serve with potato wedges (follow our chip recipe on page 34, cutting the potatoes into wedges instead) and your favourite vegetables or salad.

bangers and mash
with onion gravy

serves 4

Free

❄

ready in 45 minutes

650g potatoes, peeled and cut into chunks

350g swede, peeled and cut into chunks

salt and freshly ground black pepper

low calorie cooking spray

3 onions, thinly sliced

8 Slimming World Syn-free Pork Sausages (available from Iceland stores)

300ml boiling chicken stock

1 tbsp Worcestershire sauce

½ tsp mustard powder

2 tsp sweetener

leaves of 2 fresh thyme sprigs

Plump pork sausages, rich gravy and a big pillow of comforting mash make this a staple on every gastropub menu – and our lighter version will be a regular on your table too!

Preheat the grill to medium-high.

Boil the potatoes and swede in lightly salted boiling water for 15-20 minutes or until tender. Drain, leaving 3-4 tablespoons of the water in the pan. Season, mash until smooth and keep warm.

Meanwhile, spray a non-stick frying pan with low calorie cooking spray and place over a medium heat. Add the onions and stir-fry for 15 minutes or until they soften and turn golden.

Cook the sausages according to the packet instructions.

Add the stock to the onions along with the Worcestershire sauce, mustard powder, sweetener and most of the thyme leaves. Season and boil for 10 minutes or until the liquid has reduced by half, stirring occasionally.

Divide the mash between shallow bowls, top with the sausages and spoon over the onion gravy. Grind over a little black pepper, scatter the remaining thyme leaves and serve hot with your favourite vegetables.

If you can't get Slimming World sausages, use other low fat sausages and count the Syns – visit www.slimmingworld.co.uk for the latest information.

slow-cooked gammon
with parsley sauce

If you love bacon you'll love gammon – the saltiness of the meat goes brilliantly with the creaminess of the sauce.

Soak the gammon joint in cold water overnight (this helps reduce the saltiness).

Drain and rinse the joint and place in a large heavy-based saucepan with the stock, vegetables, peppercorns and herbs. Add enough water to cover and bring to the boil over a high heat. Reduce the heat to low and simmer gently for 2 hours 30 minutes or until the meat is very tender, topping up with water if it needs a little more.

About 15 minutes before the gammon is done, put all the parsley sauce ingredients into a food processor and blend until smooth. Heat gently to warm the sauce but be careful not to let it boil and split.

Drain the gammon and discard the vegetables (you can keep the liquid to use as stock).

Slice the gammon and serve with the parsley sauce and your favourite potatoes and vegetables.

For a cheesier parsley sauce, add 2 level tablespoons of freshly grated Parmesan cheese (½ Syn per serving) to the food processor along with the other ingredients.

serves 4

Free

ready in 2 hours 45 minutes, plus overnight soaking

800g smoked boneless gammon joint, visible fat removed

1 litre boiling chicken stock

2 onions, halved

2 carrots, peeled and cut into chunks

4 celery sticks, roughly chopped

2 tsp black peppercorns

1 bay leaf

a few thyme sprigs

for the parsley sauce

150g quark

200g fat free natural fromage frais

3 tbsp chicken stock

1 garlic clove, crushed

large handful of fresh parsley

the
full breakfast

serves 2

Free

ready in 25 minutes

2 potatoes,
peeled and cubed

4 Slimming World Syn-free
Pork Sausages (available
from Iceland stores)

low calorie cooking spray

2 tomatoes, halved

200g button mushrooms,
sliced or halved if large

1 onion, sliced into rings

4 back bacon rashers,
visible fat removed,
cut into thick strips

2 eggs

400g can baked beans

salt and freshly ground
black pepper

small handful of roughly
chopped fresh parsley

A good fry-up will fill you up all morning and maybe even longer! You'll find variations of the classic full breakfast all around the UK and Ireland – look out for extras like black pudding in England, haggis in Scotland, potato farls in Ireland and laverbread (seaweed patties) in Wales!

Preheat the grill to high.

Cook the potatoes in lightly salted boiling water for 10 minutes then drain well.

Meanwhile, cook the sausages according to the packet instructions.

Spray a large non-stick frying pan with a little low calorie cooking spray and place over a medium heat. Add the tomatoes, mushrooms, onion, bacon and potatoes and fry everything for about 5-10 minutes, turning as required, or until the vegetables are tender and the bacon is cooked.

At the same time, spray another non-stick frying pan with low calorie cooking spray and place over a medium heat. Cook the eggs for 5 minutes or until done to your liking.

Heat the baked beans in a small saucepan.

Divide everything between warmed plates (beans on the side if you prefer), season and scatter over the parsley. Serve with ketchup (1 Syn per level tablespoon) and a piping hot cuppa!

If you can't get Slimming World sausages, use other low fat sausages and count the Syns – visit www.slimmingworld.co.uk for the latest information.

liver, bacon
and onions

If you think you don't like liver, try calves' liver – it tastes amazing and has a fantastic melt-in-the-mouth texture when cooked briefly. Fresh sage adds a wonderful fragrance too, making this a traditional dish to savour.

Rinse the liver and pat dry with kitchen paper. Slice thickly, season well with salt and pepper and set aside.

Place a large non-stick frying pan over a medium heat and spray with low calorie cooking spray. Add the onion and sage and stir-fry for 4-5 minutes or until soft and lightly browned. Add the stock and bring to the boil, then lower the heat and leave to simmer gently until reduced and slightly thickened.

Place another large non-stick frying pan over a medium heat and spray with low calorie cooking spray. Add the bacon and stir-fry for 1-2 minutes, then remove with a slotted spoon and add to the onions.

Add the liver to the pan you used for the bacon and fry for 1-2 minutes on each side or until lightly browned on the outside but pink in the middle (for medium-rare, cook for 2-3 minutes on each side).

Arrange the liver on a big pile of mashed potatoes and vegetables of your choice. Pour over the onion gravy and season to serve.

serves 4

Free

❄

ready in 25 minutes

400g calves' or lambs' liver

salt and freshly ground black pepper

low calorie cooking spray

1 large onion, thinly sliced

8 fresh sage leaves, shredded

300ml boiling beef or lamb stock

4 back bacon rashers, visible fat removed, roughly chopped

roast chicken
with lemon and rosemary

serves 4

½ Syn per serving

❄

ready in 2 hours

Whether you prefer breast, thigh, drumsticks or wings, roast chicken is hard to resist… especially when it's infused with the irresistible aromas of lemon and rosemary.

1 lemon, halved

2 fresh rosemary sprigs, plus extra to garnish

1 whole chicken, about 1.2kg

low calorie cooking spray

salt and freshly ground black pepper

300ml boiling chicken stock

1 level tsp chicken gravy granules

Preheat your oven to 180°C/Fan 160°C/Gas 4.

Tuck the lemon and rosemary inside the chicken and place it in a roasting tin. Lightly spray with low calorie cooking spray and season well. Roast for 1 hour 30 minutes, spooning over the juices from time to time, or until the chicken is cooked and the juices run clear when the thickest part of the leg is pierced with a metal skewer. Remove the chicken from the oven, cover with foil and leave to rest in a warm place for 10-15 minutes.

Meanwhile, make the gravy. Put the stock in a pan and bring to the boil. Stir in the gravy granules and simmer for 3-4 minutes or until slightly thickened.

Remove the chicken skin, drain off all of the fat and carve the meat. Garnish with the extra rosemary sprigs and serve with the gravy, roast potatoes and your favourite vegetables.

fish and chips

serves 4

Free

ready in 35 minutes

6 large baking potatoes,
peeled and cut into chips

low calorie cooking spray

4 skinless cod or
haddock fillets

salt and freshly ground
black pepper

2 eggs, separated

lemon wedges, to serve

Believe it or not, neither battered fish nor chips were invented here… but we definitely came up with the idea of serving them together! Amazingly, this delicious dinner is Free!

Preheat the oven to 200°C/Fan 180°C/Gas 6.

Boil the chips in lightly salted boiling water for 5 minutes. Drain well, return to the pan and cover. Leave to cool slightly then shake the pan to roughen the edges a little.

Line a baking tray with non-stick baking parchment and arrange the chips in a single layer. Spray with low calorie cooking spray and bake for 20 minutes or until golden.

Meanwhile, arrange the fish fillets on another baking tray lined with non-stick baking parchment.

Whisk the egg whites in a large bowl until they form soft peaks. Whisk the yolks in another bowl, add a pinch of salt and fold into the egg whites. Spoon the egg mixture over the fish and bake for 12-15 minutes or until the egg is lightly browned and the fish is cooked through.

Season the fish and chips and serve with tartare sauce (see tip below), mushy peas (page 90) and lemon wedges to squeeze over.

For a quick tartare sauce, mix together four roughly chopped gherkins, a finely chopped small red onion, 1 tablespoon of capers, 2 tablespoons of extra-light mayonnaise, 200g fat free fromage frais, 1 tablespoon of finely grated unwaxed lemon zest, a little chopped dill and some seasoning (½ Syn per serving, based on four servings).

ocean pie

serves 4

½ **Syn** per serving

❄ (without the quark)

ready in 1 hour

Being surrounded by water means we have a fantastic range of fresh fish and seafood available and this rich and satisfying pie really makes the most of this incredible abundance.

1kg potatoes, peeled and chopped

2 heaped tbsp quark

salt and freshly ground black pepper

low calorie cooking spray

2 leeks, roughly chopped

350ml fish stock

300g skinless salmon fillet, cut into bite-sized pieces

300g skinless haddock fillet, cut into bite-sized pieces

200g cooked and peeled prawns

small handful of roughly chopped fresh parsley

2 level tsp cornflour

Cook the potatoes in lightly salted boiling water for 12-15 minutes or until tender and drain well. Mash the potatoes, mix in the quark and season well. Cover and set aside.

Meanwhile, spray a non-stick frying pan with low calorie cooking spray and fry the leeks over a low heat for 15 minutes or until softened.

Preheat the oven to 200°C/Fan 180°C/Gas 6.

Put the stock in a saucepan and bring to a simmer. Add the salmon and haddock and cook over a low heat for 5 minutes. Using a slotted spoon, transfer the fish to a large, shallow, ovenproof dish. Add the prawns and parsley to the fish and gently mix together.

Strain the fish stock into a clean pan and place over a high heat. Mix the cornflour with 1 tablespoon of cold water and add to the stock. Bring to the boil, reduce the heat to low and cook for 2 minutes. Add the leeks and pour the stock mixture over the fish. Gently mix everything together and season well.

Top the fish with the mashed potatoes, smooth down with a fork and bake for 20-25 minutes or until nicely browned.

Divide the pie between plates and serve with your favourite vegetables.

local heroes

Discover the dishes that are forever linked to a particular place and give the locals something to be very proud of. Some of these recipes are well known and some are hidden gems – all are totally delicious and fully Food Optimised!

ENGLAND

lancashire hotpot

serves 4

½ **Syn** per serving

❄

ready in 2 hours

low calorie cooking spray

800g lean lamb leg steaks, visible fat removed, cut into bite-sized pieces

3 onions, roughly chopped

4 celery sticks, roughly chopped

4 carrots, peeled and roughly chopped

1 level tbsp plain flour

1 tbsp Worcestershire sauce

4 tbsp tomato purée

500ml boiling lamb stock

2 bay leaves

800g potatoes, peeled and thinly sliced

salt and freshly ground black pepper

This succulent, slow-cooked classic is a fantastic family dinner, with a crispy sliced potato topping that tastes every bit as good as it looks.

Preheat your oven to 160°C/Fan 140°C/Gas 3.

Place a large ovenproof casserole pan over a high heat and spray with low calorie cooking spray. Cook the lamb in batches for 3-4 minutes or until lightly browned. Transfer each batch to a plate with a slotted spoon, cover and set aside.

Add the onions, celery and carrots to the casserole pan and stir-fry for 3-4 minutes. Sprinkle over the flour and cook for a further 2 minutes. Add the Worcestershire sauce, tomato purée and stock, and bring to the boil.

Return the lamb to the casserole pan, stir in the bay leaves and remove from the heat.

Arrange the potatoes in a spiral pattern on top of the meat and vegetables, season well and spray with low calorie cooking spray. Cover and cook in the oven for 1 hour 30 minutes or until the potatoes and lamb are tender.

Turn the heat up to 200°C/Fan 180°C/Gas 6 and spray the potatoes with low calorie cooking spray. Uncover and cook for a further 10 minutes until golden, and serve hot with your favourite vegetables.

ENGLAND

pease pudding and gammon

serves 4

Free

❄

ready in 2 hours 15 minutes, plus soaking

300g dried yellow split peas

1kg lean smoked gammon joint, visible fat removed

low calorie cooking spray

2 tbsp finely chopped fresh thyme leaves

2 onions, finely chopped

150ml boiling vegetable stock

large handful of chopped fresh parsley, stalks reserved

salt and freshly ground black pepper

¼ tsp freshly grated nutmeg

1 egg, beaten

1 bay leaf

2 carrots, roughly chopped

4 celery sticks, roughly chopped

1 tsp black peppercorns

Simple split peas take on the rich flavour of gammon from the cooking liquor in this timeless dish from England's North East.

Rinse the split peas under cold running water. Drain and tip into a bowl, cover with boiling water and set aside to soak for 30 minutes.

Meanwhile, place the gammon in a large pan of cold water. Bring to the boil, remove from the heat and discard the water (this helps stops scum forming on the surface later on).

Spray a non-stick saucepan with low calorie cooking spray, add the thyme and half the onions and cook over a low heat for 5 minutes or until beginning to soften, stirring occasionally. Pour in the stock and simmer for a further 10 minutes or until all the stock has been absorbed.

Drain the split peas and add to the onion mixture. Pour in 1 litre of cold water, turn the heat to high and bring to the boil. Turn the heat to low and simmer for 35 minutes or until the split peas are tender and the liquid has nearly all been absorbed. Remove from the heat and blend to a thick purée. Add most of the chopped parsley to the purée, season to taste and stir in the nutmeg and beaten egg.

Spoon the mixture into the centre of a large double layered piece of muslin and tie with kitchen string to seal into a parcel. Place the parcel into the saucepan alongside the gammon. Cover completely with cold water. Add the parsley stalks, bay leaf, carrots, celery, black peppercorns and remaining onion to the water. Bring to the boil then cover, turn the heat to low and simmer for 1 hour.

Lift the gammon and pease pudding from the cooking liquid with a slotted spoon (you can strain the liquid and use it as stock). Untie the pudding and divide between plates. Scatter over the remaining parsley and serve with slices of gammon and your favourite vegetables.

You can buy muslin in the baking departments of large supermarkets, cookshops or online. Don't worry if you can't find any – a clean tea towel will also do the job.

ENGLAND

scouse

serves 4

Free

❄

ready in 2 hours 45 minutes

---

low calorie cooking spray

350g lean beef steak, visible fat removed, cut into chunks

350g lean lamb leg steak, visible fat removed, cut into chunks

salt and freshly ground black pepper

600ml boiling beef stock

2 onions, roughly chopped

4 carrots, peeled and sliced

2 tsp dried mixed herbs

2 tbsp Worcestershire sauce

900g potatoes, peeled and cut into chunks

Tuck into a filling bowlful of the hearty stew that gives Liverpudlians their nickname! This dish was actually brought here by sailors from Northern Europe, who slow-cooked cheap cuts like scrag end lamb – we've used lean beef and lamb leg steaks to make it Free!

Preheat the oven to 180°C/Fan 160°C/Gas 4.

Spray low calorie cooking spray into a large heavy-based casserole pan (that has a tight-fitting lid) and place over a medium heat. Season the meat with salt and pepper and cook in batches until browned all over. Return all the meat to the casserole dish.

Stir in the stock, onions, carrots, dried herbs and Worcestershire sauce then cover and cook for 1 hour 30 minutes.

Scatter the potatoes over the meat, pushing them into the stock. Season, cover and cook for a further 1 hour or until the meat and vegetables are tender.

Remove a few potato chunks, mash until smooth and return to the casserole to help thicken the sauce.

Serve this tasty stew hot with your favourite vegetables.

omelette
arnold bennett

This famous dish was created for the English novelist Arnold Bennett by the chefs at the Savoy Hotel in London, where it is still on the menu today! The original recipe is quite fiddly and high in Syns so we've made it much simpler and lighter.

serves 1 as a main meal
or 2 as a starter

1½ Syns per serving
(based on 1 serving)

ready in 25 minutes

110g smoked haddock, skinned

100ml skimmed milk

1 bay leaf

1 tsp black peppercorns

2 tbsp fat free
natural fromage frais

finely grated zest
of ½ unwaxed lemon

freshly ground black pepper

low calorie cooking spray

3 large eggs, beaten

a few roughly chopped
fresh chives

Preheat the grill to hot.

Put the fish into a small saucepan just large enough for it to fit snugly. Pour over the milk and add the bay leaf and peppercorns. Bring to the boil, turn the heat to low and poach for 3-4 minutes. Turn off the heat, cover and set aside for 5 minutes.

Mix together the fromage frais and lemon zest in a bowl. Lift the fish from the poaching liquid with a slotted spoon, flake into the fromage frais mixture and season with freshly ground black pepper. Strain the poaching liquid into a bowl and set aside.

Spray a non-stick frying pan with low calorie cooking spray and place over a low heat. Beat the eggs, add half of the poaching liquid (discarding the rest) and whisk to combine. Pour the eggs into the pan and draw the edges of the omelette into the centre as it begins to set. Cook for 1-2 minutes or until the omelette is set on the bottom and slightly soft on the top.

Spread the fish mixture over the omelette and grill for 2-3 minutes or until set.

Scatter over the chives, grind over a little more pepper and serve hot with salad or your favourite veg.

For an even more authentic and luxurious omelette Arnold Bennett, sprinkle 1 level tablespoon of freshly grated Parmesan cheese just before grilling (adds 1 Syn to the whole omelette).

ENGLAND

pan haggerty

serves 4

Free

ready in 45 minutes

1kg potatoes, peeled and cut into bite-sized pieces

½ green cabbage, shredded

low calorie cooking spray

2 onions, halved and finely sliced

2 garlic cloves, crushed

225g lean ham, visible fat removed, diced

2 eggs, lightly beaten

salt and freshly ground black pepper

This hearty potato and onion cake from the North East of England is an amazingly low-cost dinner – our version includes cabbage and tasty ham to make it a complete meal.

Cook the potatoes in a saucepan of lightly salted boiling water for about 10-12 minutes or until just tender, adding the cabbage for the last 4 minutes. Drain, return to the saucepan and leave to cool.

Meanwhile, spray a large non-stick ovenproof frying pan with low calorie cooking spray and place over a low-medium heat. Add the onions and fry for 10 minutes, adding the garlic for the last 2 minutes.

Preheat the oven to 180°C/Fan 160°C/Gas 4.

Add the onions and garlic to the potatoes and cabbage in the saucepan and stir in the ham and eggs. Season and mix well.

Spray the ovenproof frying pan with more low calorie cooking spray and spoon in the potato mixture, pressing down lightly. Fry for 5 minutes over a medium heat then transfer the frying pan to the oven and bake for 20 minutes or until lightly golden.

This is delicious served hot with salad.

english
crab salad

Eating fresh crab is a highlight on a trip to the seaside
– and British fishermen catch some of the world's best,
most famously off Cromer on the Norfolk coast. In this
refreshing Free salad we've combined juicy fruit and
soft, sweet crab – ideal for a special occasion starter
or a light lunch.

In a large bowl, mix the lemon zest, fromage frais and 1 tablespoon of
vinaigrette. Season to taste with salt and freshly ground black pepper then
gently stir in the crab meat, chilli and tarragon.

Toss the celery, pears, watercress and red chicory in the lemon juice and
remaining vinaigrette and pile on to four plates. Spoon dollops of the crab
mixture over the salad to serve.

If you can't find fresh crab meat, canned crab is just as tasty!

serves 4

Free

ready in 20 minutes

---

finely grated zest and
juice of ½ small unwaxed
lemon

1 tbsp fat free
natural fromage frais

4 tbsp fat free vinaigrette

salt and freshly ground
black pepper

240g fresh white crab meat
or 2 x 170g cans white
crab meat, drained

1 red chilli, deseeded
and finely chopped

2 tsp finely chopped
fresh tarragon

2 celery sticks,
trimmed and thinly sliced

2 ripe pears, peeled, halved,
cored and thinly sliced

small bag of watercress

1 head of red chicory,
trimmed, leaves separated

ENGLAND

faggots
with onion gravy

serves 4

1½ Syns per serving

❄

ready in 1 hour

175g pigs' liver,
sinew trimmed

500g lean pork mince
(5% fat or less)

50g wholemeal bread,
crumbed

1 tbsp finely chopped
fresh sage

salt and freshly ground
black pepper

low calorie cooking spray

2 onions, thinly sliced

350ml boiling beef stock

1 level tbsp cornflour

When times were hard, creative British cooks turned to offal to make economical dishes that were just as tasty and satisfying as prime cuts of meat. Faggots are thought to have been created in the Midlands before catching on in Wales and the West Country.

Preheat the oven to 200°C/Fan 180°C/Gas 6.

Put the pigs' liver into a food processor and whizz to chop roughly. Add the mince, breadcrumbs and half the sage and whizz again until well combined. Season well with salt and freshly ground black pepper and transfer to a bowl. Using wet hands, shape the mixture into 20 equal-sized faggots.

Spray a roasting tin with low calorie cooking spray and spread out the onions over the base. Spray with a little more low calorie cooking spray, arrange the faggots over the top and bake for 20 minutes.

Pour over the beef stock and sprinkle with the remaining sage, then cover with foil and bake for a further 20 minutes. Mix the cornflour with 1 tablespoon of cold water to make a smooth paste and stir into the sauce – it should thicken instantly.

Divide the faggots and onions between plates and serve hot with your favourite potatoes and veg.

We served the faggots with a satisfying carrot and swede mash. Peel and roughly chop 500g each of swede and carrots and cook in lightly salted boiling water for 15-20 minutes. Drain well and mash until smooth.

ENGLAND

london
particular soup

serves 4

Free

❄ (without the
fromage frais)

ready in 1 hour 30 minutes

This filling and flavoursome soup was invented to
help Londoners cope with the chill of a thick fog
(or 'pea-souper') but it's guaranteed to keep the
cold at bay wherever you live!

low calorie cooking spray

1 onion, roughly chopped

1 carrot, peeled
and roughly chopped

2 celery sticks, trimmed
and roughly chopped

225g dried split peas
(unsoaked)

1.2 litres boiling
chicken stock

225g slice of smoked lean
ham, visible fat removed

freshly ground black pepper

small handful of roughly
chopped fresh parsley

4 tbsp fat free natural
fromage frais

Place a large heavy-based saucepan over a medium heat and spray with
low calorie cooking spray. Add the onion, carrot and celery and cook for
4-5 minutes, stirring often, until beginning to soften. Add the split peas and
stock. Bring to the boil then turn the heat to low and simmer for 50 minutes.
Add the slice of ham and simmer for a further 15-20 minutes or until the peas
are tender.

Leave to cool slightly then lift out the ham and shred with two forks. Set aside.

Blitz the pea mixture with a stick blender until smooth, adding a little boiling
water to get the consistency you want. Season to taste with freshly ground
black pepper and stir in most of the ham and parsley.

Divide the soup between mugs or bowls and add a dollop of fromage frais to
each one. Scatter with the remaining ham and parsley and serve hot.

WALES

glamorgan sausages

serves 4

Free

❄ Ⓥ

ready in 45 minutes,
plus chilling

This clever twist on the famous Welsh vegetarian dish shows that sausages don't need to be meaty to be magnificent! These flavoursome bangers come with a rich, rustic tomato sauce and are a treat with lots of creamy mash.

2 x 400g cans cannellini beans, drained and rinsed

1 small red onion, finely chopped

large handful of roughly chopped fresh parsley

4 carrots, peeled and grated

2 tsp dried mixed herbs

a splash of Tabasco sauce

low calorie cooking spray

for the sauce

250g passata with herbs

1 tbsp balsamic vinegar

1 tbsp sweetener

salt and freshly ground black pepper

First make the sauce. Put the passata in a small saucepan with the balsamic vinegar and sweetener and season well. Bring to the boil then turn the heat to low, cover and simmer very gently for 4-5 minutes, stirring often. Set aside to cool.

Meanwhile, pop the beans into a food processor with the onion, parsley, carrots, mixed herbs and Tabasco sauce. Season to taste and pulse to combine. Transfer the mixture to a mixing bowl, cover and chill for 3-4 hours (this will help the sausages hold their shape when you cook them).

Divide the bean mixture into 12 equal portions and form each one into a sausage. Spray a large non-stick frying pan with low calorie cooking spray and place over a high heat. Cook the sausages for 5-6 minutes or until lightly browned and crisp, turning occasionally. (You might need to do this in batches.)

Serve the sausages hot with the tomato sauce, mashed potatoes and your favourite vegetables.

cawl

WALES

You get two courses for the price of one with the amazing national dish of Wales: a warming broth to enjoy as a starter plus a more-ish main course of tender meat and vegetables. Pudding not included!

serves 4

Free

❄

ready in 3 hours

Preheat the oven to 180°C/Fan 160°C/Gas 4.

Spray a large non-stick frying pan with low calorie cooking spray and place over a medium heat. Fry the onions, carrots, swede and leeks for 5 minutes or until lightly coloured, stirring occasionally. Tip into a large heavy-based casserole dish (with a tight-fitting lid).

Spray the frying pan with a little more low calorie cooking spray and fry the lamb and bacon in batches, adding the browned meat to the vegetables in the casserole dish (a good colour on your meat will add a lot of flavour to your stock). Season with salt and freshly ground black pepper and stir well. Tuck in the bay leaf and thyme sprigs and pour over just enough cold water to cover. Put the lid on and cook in the oven for around 2½ hours or until the lamb and vegetables are tender.

Drain most of the cooking liquid (about 1.2 litres) into a separate pan and keep warm to serve as a starter.

Crumble the stock cube over the lamb and stir in, then check the seasoning and keep warm.

Serve the soup first, followed by the tasty meat and vegetables.

The soup is traditionally quite thin but you could mash in a few of the veggies if you prefer a thicker consistency.

low calorie cooking spray

2 onions, roughly chopped

3 carrots, peeled and cut into chunks

1 swede, peeled and cut into chunks

2 leeks, trimmed and thickly sliced

700g lean lamb leg steaks, visible fat removed, cut into chunks

4 back bacon rashers, visible fat removed, roughly chopped

salt and freshly ground black pepper

1 bay leaf

3 fresh thyme sprigs

1 lamb stock cube

beef mince 'haggis' with neeps and tatties

Haggis is eaten with neeps (mashed turnip or swede) and tatties (mashed potatoes) all year round in Scotland – and especially to celebrate the life of the poet Robert Burns on Burns Night (25 January). Our low-Syn version uses lean beef mince and just a small amount of offal, making it much easier to cook at home.

Spray a large non-stick frying pan with low calorie cooking spray and place over a high heat. Add the beef, bacon and chicken liver and cook for 5 minutes, stirring frequently. Add the onion, thyme, spices and ½ teaspoon of freshly ground black pepper and cook for a further 2-3 minutes.

Pour the stock over the beef mixture and bring to the boil. Turn the heat to low and simmer for 15 minutes until the stock has been absorbed. Season to taste and stir in the porridge oats.

Meanwhile, cook the turnips or swede in a pan of lightly salted boiling water for 15 minutes. Cook the potatoes in another pan of lightly salted boiling water for 12-15 minutes.

Drain the potatoes, return to the pan with the fromage frais and mash until smooth and creamy. Drain the turnips or swede and return to a gentle heat to drive off any excess moisture. Scatter the turnips or swede with parsley and season to taste (you can mash this too, if you like).

Serve the haggis hot with the tatties and neeps – and if it's Burns Night, don't forget to toast Rabbie Burns!

For even tastier tatties, stir in 1 level tablespoon of creamed horseradish with the fromage frais (½ Syn per serving).

serves 4

1½ Syns per serving

❄ (without the fromage frais)

ready in 40 minutes

___

low calorie cooking spray

500g lean beef mince (5% fat or less)

4 back bacon rashers, visible fat removed, finely chopped

200g chicken liver, trimmed of any sinew, finely chopped

1 large onion, finely chopped

1 tbsp fresh thyme leaves

½ tsp ground allspice

large pinch of ground cloves

large pinch of freshly grated nutmeg

salt and freshly ground black pepper

200ml boiling beef stock

35g porridge oats

2 turnips or 1 swede, peeled and cut into chunks

1kg floury potatoes, peeled and cut into chunks

2 tbsp fat free natural fromage frais

small handful of finely chopped fresh parsley

SCOTLAND

serves 4

Free

❄

ready in 2½ hours

low calorie cooking spray

4 skinless and boneless chicken breasts, thickly sliced

4 back bacon rashers, visible fat removed, roughly chopped

1 tbsp all-purpose seasoning

850g potatoes, peeled and thinly sliced

2 onions, thinly sliced

salt and freshly ground black pepper

2 tbsp chopped fresh thyme

2 medium carrots, thinly sliced

350ml boiling chicken stock

stovied chicken
and potatoes

Stovies is a fantastic Scottish dish designed for using up leftover meat and vegetables by slow-cooking them in a sealed pot with potatoes and onions. We've used fresh ingredients for convenience but in the spirit of the recipe, swap in leftovers wherever you can!

Preheat the oven to 150°C/Fan 130°C/Gas 2.

Spray a large non-stick frying pan with low calorie cooking spray and place over a low-medium heat. Add the chicken, bacon and all-purpose seasoning and fry for 5 minutes or until lightly browned, stirring frequently.

Arrange half the potatoes in a heavy-based casserole dish (that has a tight-fitting lid) then add a layer using up all the onions. Season well with salt and pepper and sprinkle over the thyme. Add the chicken, bacon and carrots in a single layer and finish with a layer of potatoes. Pour over the stock and season well, then cover and cook in the oven for 1½ hours.

Remove the lid, spray with a little low calorie cooking spray and return to the oven uncovered for a further 30 minutes.

Serve hot with your favourite vegetables or salad.

For a thicker sauce, mash some of the potatoes with the back of a fork just before serving and stir in well.

dublin coddle

This hearty sausage and bacon casserole offers a warm Irish welcome to anyone coming in from the cold!

serves 4

Free

❄

ready in 1 hour 45 minutes

Preheat the oven to 200°C/Fan 180°C/Gas 6.

Spray a large non-stick frying pan with low calorie cooking spray and place over a medium heat. Fry the onions for 5 minutes or until golden and beginning to soften. Add the bacon and sausages and fry for a further 5 minutes or until the sausages are browned and the onions have caramelised, adding a little stock if the pan is looking a bit dry. Halve the sausages and return to the pan.

Spoon the sausage mixture into a large casserole dish (that has a tight-fitting lid). Arrange the potatoes on top, slightly overlapping, to completely cover the sausage mixture. Pour over the stock and push the potatoes down into the stock. Season with salt and pepper, cover and bake for 45 minutes.

Lower the heat to 180°C/Fan 160°C/Gas 4. Spray the potatoes with a little low calorie cooking spray and cook uncovered for a further 30 minutes.

Serve hot with your favourite vegetables.

If you can't get Slimming World sausages, use other low fat sausages and count the Syns – visit www.slimmingworld.co.uk for the latest information.

low calorie cooking spray

2 large onions, thinly sliced

8 back bacon rashers, visible fat removed, roughly chopped

8 Slimming World Syn-free Pork Sausages (available from Iceland stores)

550ml boiling beef stock

650g potatoes, peeled and thinly sliced

salt and freshly ground black pepper

IRELAND

irish stew

serves 4

1 Syn per serving

❄

ready in 2 hours 15 minutes

Apart from the amazing flavours, the best thing about this classic lamb stew from the Emerald Isle is its simplicity. Just pop it all into a casserole pan and let your hob do the rest!

700g lean lamb leg steaks, visible fat removed, cut into large chunks

3 onions, thickly sliced

2 garlic cloves, crushed

2 turnips or 1 swede, peeled and roughly chopped

4 carrots, peeled and roughly chopped

4 celery sticks, roughly chopped

900ml boiling chicken stock

1 tbsp chicken gravy granules

salt and freshly ground black pepper

Put the lamb, onions, garlic, turnips or swede, carrots and celery in a large heavy-based casserole pan. Add the stock and gravy granules, mix well and bring to the boil over a high heat.

Season well and cover tightly then turn the heat to very low and cook for 2 hours or until the lamb is very tender.

Serve hot with your favourite potatoes and vegetables.

...and two veg

Whatever you're having for dinner, you're spoilt for choice when it comes to choosing your side vegetables. These simple recipes really make the most of the UK and Ireland's sensational produce – you'll never forget your roots again!

colcannon

serves 4

Free

Ⓥ

ready in 25 minutes

This eternally popular Irish side dish makes simple mashed potatoes and cabbage much more of a treat by mixing them together!

1kg potatoes, peeled and cut into chunks

½ Savoy cabbage, cored and shredded

100g fat free natural fromage frais

salt and freshly ground black pepper

Cook the potatoes in a pan of lightly salted boiling water for 12-15 minutes, adding the cabbage for the last 5 minutes to soften the leaves. Drain and return to a low heat to drive off any excess moisture.

Remove the pan from the heat, stir in the fromage frais and mash until smooth. Season to taste and serve hot.

To make champ, another Irish favourite, swap the cabbage for a bunch of finely chopped spring onions.

The old British favourite bubble and squeak is a great way to use up leftover veg. Spray a pan with low calorie cooking spray, add mashed potatoes, 1 teaspoon of mustard powder and some cooked cabbage (plus any other leftover veg you fancy) and fry until nicely browned.

cauliflower cheese

serves 4

3½ Syns per serving

Ⓥ

ready in 40 minutes,
plus standing

2 cauliflowers,
broken into florets

low calorie cooking spray

bunch of spring onions,
thinly sliced

2 garlic cloves, chopped

500g fat free natural yogurt

1 level tsp English mustard

2 eggs, lightly beaten

90g reduced fat Cheddar
cheese, coarsely grated

salt and freshly ground
black pepper

Give cauliflower a cheese and mustard makeover with this easy version of the all-time classic. Serve with a crisp salad to make a main course or as a luxurious side dish with fish or chicken.

Cook the cauliflower florets in a saucepan of lightly salted boiling water for 7-8 minutes then drain and tip into an ovenproof dish.

Meanwhile, spray a large non-stick frying pan with low calorie cooking spray and place over a high heat. Add the spring onions and garlic and cook for 2-3 minutes.

Preheat the oven to 220°C/Fan 200°C/Gas 7.

Put the yogurt, mustard, eggs and two-thirds of the cheese into a bowl. Add the spring onions and garlic, season well and mix together to combine all of those great flavours. Pour the mixture over the cauliflower, sprinkle with the remaining cheese and bake for 15-20 minutes or until lightly golden and bubbling.

Remove from the heat and leave to stand for 5 minutes before serving warm.

roast
potatoes

It's hard to imagine British food without the potato! Filling, tasty and incredibly versatile, they're perhaps at their very best roasted and served with a juicy joint of meat.

serves 4

Free

❄ Ⓥ

ready in 50 minutes

1kg floury potatoes such as Maris Piper, peeled and cut to the size you like

low calorie cooking spray

2 tsp garlic salt (optional)

small handful of finely chopped fresh thyme leaves

Preheat the oven to 220°C/Fan 200°C/Gas 7 and line a roasting tin with non-stick baking parchment.

Cook the potatoes in a pan of lightly salted boiling water for 6-8 minutes or until they're just starting to soften. Drain thoroughly and tip the potatoes into the roasting tin.

Spray the potatoes with low calorie cooking spray and sprinkle over the garlic salt, if using. Scatter over the thyme and roast at the top of the oven for 25-30 minutes or until crisp and golden on the outside and tender inside.

Serve hot with your favourite roast.

asparagus, poached eggs
and hollandaise sauce

serves 4

½ **Syn** per serving

Ⓥ

ready in 20 minutes

600g asparagus spears,
trimmed

1 tbsp white wine vinegar

4 eggs*

for the hollandaise sauce

2 tbsp extra-light
mayonnaise

100g fat free natural
fromage frais

finely grated zest and
juice of ½ unwaxed lemon,
plus wedges to serve
(optional)

3 tbsp warm vegetable
stock or water

salt and freshly ground
black pepper

*Pregnant women, the
elderly and babies are
advised not to eat raw or
partially cooked eggs.*

Britain produces some of the best asparagus in
the world and it makes a fantastic starter or light
lunch topped with a softly poached egg. (We know
hollandaise is French but there's nothing quite as
delicious with asparagus!)

Cook the asparagus spears in a saucepan of lightly salted boiling water for
8-10 minutes or until just tender.

Meanwhile, put all the hollandaise ingredients in a bowl, season and whisk well.

Bring another saucepan of water to a simmer. Add the vinegar and stir the
water quickly to create a whirlpool (this helps keep the eggs together). Crack
two of the eggs into the water and poach for about 2-3 minutes, then lift out of
the pan using a slotted spoon, drain on kitchen paper and keep warm. Repeat
with the other two eggs.

Drain the asparagus and divide between plates. Top with a poached egg and
serve with plenty of hollandaise sauce, a good grind of black pepper and
lemon wedges, if you like.

jersey royal
potato salad

This delicious potato variety is Jersey's finest export and the unique flavour is best shown off in a satisfying salad. They're in season in spring and early summer but don't worry if you can't find them, as new potatoes will work just as well.

Boil the potatoes in a saucepan of lightly salted boiling water for 10-12 minutes or until tender, then drain and put them into a large mixing bowl.

Meanwhile, mix all the dressing ingredients in a bowl and season well.

Pour the dressing over the potatoes and set aside to cool. Add the apples and celery, toss well and serve cold.

serves 4

Free

🅥

ready in 20 minutes

1kg Jersey Royals or new potatoes, scrubbed and halved

3 red apples, cored and cut into thin wedges

4 celery sticks, thinly sliced

for the dressing

300g fat free natural fromage frais

½ tsp mustard powder

1 tbsp cider vinegar

bunch of spring onions, thinly sliced

small handful of finely chopped fresh dill

small handful of finely chopped fresh chives

salt and freshly ground black pepper

red cabbage
with red onions

serves 4

Free

✱ ⓥ

ready in 25 minutes

low calorie cooking spray

1 large red cabbage, halved, core removed, finely sliced

2 red onions, thinly sliced

salt and freshly ground black pepper

1 tsp ground cinnamon

3 tbsp red wine vinegar

juice of 1 lemon

3 tbsp sweetener (optional)

small handful of roughly chopped fresh parsley, to garnish

Red cabbage tends to make us think of Christmas but its sensational sweetness makes it a tempting side dish all year round.

Spray a large non-stick frying pan with low calorie cooking spray and place over a high heat. Add the cabbage and onions and stir-fry for 5 minutes until the cabbage has softened slightly. Season well and add the cinnamon, vinegar and lemon juice.

Stir-fry for a further 5-6 minutes until the cabbage is just tender but still has a bit of bite. Stir in the sweetener, if using, and scatter over the parsley to serve.

This speedy dish gives cabbage with a bit of crunch. If you prefer your cabbage to be more tender, add 200ml of water, cover and simmer for an extra 15 minutes.

minted
mushy peas

serves 4

Free

ⓥ

ready in 10 minutes

Fish and chips wouldn't be the same without a big bowl of mushy peas on the side. They're often made with plumper marrowfat peas but our version uses regular peas and mint for a fresher flavour.

500g frozen peas

100g fat free natural fromage frais

half a bunch of spring onions, trimmed

small handful of fresh mint leaves

salt and freshly ground black pepper

Cook the peas according to the packet instructions and drain thoroughly.

Put the peas into a food processor along with the fromage frais and most of the spring onions and mint leaves. Season well and blitz to the consistency you want.

Transfer to a serving bowl, stir in the remaining spring onions and scatter over the remaining mint leaves to serve.

Another delicious way to serve peas is with mint and lemon. Cook the peas according to the packet instructions, drain and add a small handful of finely chopped fresh mint and the juice of a lemon.

rumbledethumps

serves 4

2½ Syns per serving

Ⓥ

ready in 1 hour

½ Savoy cabbage, shredded

1 onion, roughly chopped

600g turnips or swede, peeled and diced

800g potatoes, peeled and diced

4 tbsp skimmed milk

salt and freshly ground black pepper

60g reduced fat Cheddar cheese, grated

Traditionally popular in the Scottish Borders, rumbledethumps is a mouth-watering combination of potatoes, swede or turnip, onion and cabbage, scattered with cheese and baked until golden and bubbling. We've served it in individual pots to make a satisfying side dish.

Preheat the oven to 190°C/Fan 170°C/Gas 5.

Cook the cabbage in a large pan of lightly salted boiling water for 3-4 minutes. Remove with a slotted spoon and set aside.

Return the water to the boil, add the onion and turnips or swede and cook for 5 minutes. Add the potatoes and cook for a further 8-10 minutes until nice and tender. Drain well and return to the pan. Break up some of the potatoes and turnips or swede with a fork, stir in the cabbage and milk and season to taste.

Spoon the mixture into individual ovenproof dishes or ramekins and sprinkle with the cheese. Bake for 30-35 minutes or until the tops are golden brown and serve hot with meat or chicken.

You can also shape the rumbledethump mixture into tasty cakes. When the vegetable mixture is cool enough to handle, divide it into eight equal portions and form each one into a cake. Arrange the cakes on a baking sheet sprayed lightly with low calorie cooking spray, sprinkle over the cheese and bake as above.

happy ever afters

Our puddings are the envy of the world – and whether you're after an easy Eton mess, a crunchy crumble or a luxurious lemon meringue pie, you'll find a luscious low-Syn version here.

raspberry
and apple cranachan

serves 4

2 Syns per serving

ready in 15 minutes

---

low calorie cooking spray

4 level tsp jumbo
porridge oats

2 tbsp sweetener

2 x 175g pots Muller
Light Vanilla yogurt (or
other Free vanilla yogurt)

1 apple, peeled, cored
and coarsely grated

300g raspberries

4 tbsp fat free natural
fromage frais, sweetened
to taste

Our lighter version of the creamy Scottish classic
is packed with fresh fruit, yogurt and fromage frais,
and topped with crunchy toasted oats.

Place a non-stick frying pan over a medium-high heat and spray with low calorie cooking spray. Add the oats and toast for 1 minute. Add half the sweetener and stir-fry for 2-3 minutes or until the oats are lightly browned. Transfer to a piece of non-stick baking parchment.

Meanwhile, mix together the yogurts, apple, raspberries and remaining sweetener in a bowl.

Divide the yogurt mixture between dessert glasses, top each glass with 1 tablespoon of fromage frais and scatter over the toasted oats to serve.

For an indulgent and very authentic adult twist, soak the raspberries in 35ml Scotch whisky and mix into the yogurt along with the apple (1 Syn extra per serving).

summer pudding

serves 6

2 Syns per serving

ready in 30 minutes,
plus chilling

500g frozen mixed berries,
defrosted, plus extra
to decorate

2 tbsp sweetener

6 medium slices of 2-day-old
white bread from a small
400g loaf, crusts removed

fat free natural
fromage frais, sweetened
to taste, to serve

This chilled fruity pudding is a treat on a hot day and using frozen berries makes it seriously low-cost too.

Put the berries in a bowl with the sweetener and 100ml of water. Stir well then strain into another bowl, reserving both the berries and the juice.

Line a 750ml pudding basin with cling film, letting the edges overhang by about 15cm. Cut four slices of bread in half, a little on an angle, so you have eight lopsided rectangles. Cut a further slice of bread into four triangles and leave the final slice whole.

Dip the whole slice of bread into the berry juice for a few seconds to coat, then press it into the bottom of the basin.

Next, dip one of the rectangular pieces of bread into the juice and, holding it so the narrowest edge is at the top, press it into the side of the basin. Follow with another piece, this time with the narrow edge at the bottom, so they fit snugly. Continue with the remaining rectangles all the way around the basin, trimming the last piece to fit. Spoon in the berries.

Dip the four triangles in the juice, place them on top of the pudding and trim off any overhang with scissors. Bring together the edges of the cling film and loosely seal. Put a small plate on top and weigh it down (cans work well for this), then chill for 8-10 hours or overnight if possible.

To serve, open the cling film, hold a serving plate against the top of the basin and flip it over. Lift off the basin and cling film and serve, decorated with more berries and drizzled with the remaining juice, plus a big dollop of fromage frais.

food glorious food | **happy ever afters**

gooseberry fool

serves 4

1 Syn per serving

ready in 25 minutes,
plus cooling and chilling

400g gooseberries,
topped and tailed

2 tbsp sweetener

3 x 175g pots Muller
Light Vanilla yogurt (or
other Free vanilla yogurt)

1 small egg white*

*Pregnant women, the
elderly and babies are
advised not to eat raw or
partially cooked eggs.

The contrast between creamy yogurt and slightly tart gooseberries is a winner in this low-Syn and very traditional dessert. Gooseberries are in season from June to August and become sweeter as the year goes on.

Put the gooseberries in a saucepan with 100ml of water and the sweetener. Bring to the boil over a high heat then turn the heat down to low and simmer for 10-12 minutes or until the fruit is soft and pulpy. Remove from the heat, cool completely and chill for 2-3 hours.

Put the yogurts into a mixing bowl and gently swirl through most of the gooseberry mixture.

In a separate bowl, whisk the egg white until soft peaks form then fold into the yogurt mixture with a metal spoon.

Spoon the mixture into chilled dessert bowls or glasses, swirl the remaining gooseberry mixture on top and chill for 2-3 hours before serving.

sparkling
pimm's jellies

Our sparkling jelly captures all the fun of the summer. This one is strictly for adults only!

serves 4

2 Syns per serving

ready in 25 minutes, plus cooling and chilling

Put the leaf gelatine in a bowl of cold water for 10-12 minutes or until soft.

Heat half of the lemonade in a saucepan over a high heat. When it is nearly boiling, remove from the heat.

Lift the gelatine sheets out of the water, squeeze out the excess liquid and stir the gelatine sheets into the hot lemonade until dissolved. Add the Pimm's, lime juice and remaining lemonade and set aside to cool.

Divide the orange segments and most of the blackberries between four dessert glasses. Pour in the cooled lemonade mixture and chill for 2-3 hours or until set.

Add a dollop of fromage frais to each glass and decorate with mint sprigs and the remaining blackberries.

3 sheets of leaf gelatine

400ml diet lemonade

100ml Pimm's

juice of 1 lime

3 large oranges, peeled and segmented

200g blackberries

fat free natural fromage frais, sweetened to taste

mint sprigs, to decorate

lemon
meringue pie

serves 8

4½ Syns per serving

ready in 45 minutes, plus
cooling and chilling

This eye-catching pud was everywhere in the 1960s
and 1970s and now it's back in fashion again – and
lower in Syns than ever!

1 level tsp plain flour,
for dusting

200g ready-made light
shortcrust pastry

6 sheets of leaf gelatine

finely grated zest and
juice of 2 unwaxed lemons

2 large eggs, separated*

11.5g sachet sugar-free
lemon & lime jelly crystals

3 tbsp sweetener

*Pregnant women, the
elderly and babies are
advised not to eat raw or
partially cooked eggs.*

Preheat your oven to 180°C/Fan 160°C/Gas 4.

Dust your work surface with the flour, then roll out the pastry and use it to
line a 20cm, loose-bottomed deep tart tin. Cover the pastry with baking
parchment and fill with baking beans (or dried rice). Bake for 15-20 minutes,
then remove the beans and paper and return the pastry to the oven for
5 minutes or until crisp and golden. Allow to cool in the tin.

Meanwhile, soak the gelatine in a bowl of cold water for 10-12 minutes or
until softened. Put the lemon zest and juice, egg yolks, jelly crystals and
2 tablespoons of sweetener in a pan and place over a medium heat. Add
600ml of cold water and cook, whisking continuously, for 12-15 minutes
or until the mixture starts to thicken.

Squeeze the water out of the gelatine sheets, add the sheets to the jelly
mixture and stir until dissolved. Remove from the heat and leave to cool.

Pour the cooled mixture into the cooled pastry case. Cover and chill for
6-8 hours or overnight if time allows, until firm.

When you're ready to eat, preheat the grill to medium.

Put the egg whites in a large, clean glass bowl and add the remaining
sweetener. Beat with an electric hand whisk on a medium speed until the
mixture forms stiff peaks. Spoon the egg white mixture over the lemon base
and grill for 1 minute or until lightly browned. Slice and serve straight away,
while the meringue is still holding its shape.

mixed berry
eton mess

First served at the posh English school, this more-ish dessert is bursting with summer fruits and the sweetness of crushed meringue.

Put all of the berries in a mixing bowl.

Add the yogurts and swirl through, then fold in the crushed meringue nests and spoon into four dessert glasses or teacups to serve.

You can use any fruits you like to make an Eton mess. Try a tropical mix of kiwi fruits, pineapple and mango; or an orchard version with apples and pears.

serves 4

2½ Syns per serving

ready in 10 minutes

100g blackberries

100g blueberries

100g raspberries

100g strawberries, hulled and halved or quartered if large

2 x 175g pots Muller Light Raspberry & Cranberry or Strawberry yogurt (or other Free raspberry or strawberry yogurts)

4 meringue nests, roughly crushed

rice pudding

serves 4

3 Syns per serving

🅥

ready in 2 hour 15 minutes

---

low calorie cooking spray

100g dried pudding rice

2 tbsp sweetener

650ml skimmed milk

1 tsp vanilla extract or
seeds of ½ vanilla pod

1 tsp freshly grated nutmeg,
plus extra to decorate

1 tsp ground cinnamon

The pudding so many of us remember from childhood is just as irresistible for grown-ups, and our low-Syn version is infused with appealing hints of vanilla, nutmeg and cinnamon.

Preheat your oven to 150°C/Fan 130°C/Gas 2 and lightly spray a medium baking dish with low calorie cooking spray.

Put the rice in a large sieve and rinse under cold water for 1-2 minutes. Drain and transfer to the baking dish. Add all the remaining ingredients, stir well and bake for 1 hour.

Stir the rice pudding again and return to the oven for another 30 minutes. Stir again, then bake for a further 30 minutes or until lightly browned.

Serve warm with a little grated nutmeg on top.

orange
and strawberry trifles

serves 4

4 Syns per serving

ready in 20 minutes, plus
cooling and chilling

2 x 11.5g sachets of
sugar-free strawberry
jelly crystals

300g strawberries, hulled
and halved or quartered, plus
extra sliced strawberries
to decorate

1 large orange, peeled and
split into segments

200g ready-made low-fat
custard from a can or carton

4 tbsp fat free natural
fromage frais, sweetened
to taste

1 level tsp cocoa powder,
to dust

1 level tsp icing sugar,
to dust

You'll find all the best things in life in a good trifle and
our light version includes lashings of creamy custard,
fabulous fresh fruit and a wealth of wobbly jelly.

Make the jelly according to the packet instructions and leave to cool.

Divide the strawberries and orange segments between dessert glasses.
Pour in the cooled jelly mixture, cover and chill for 6-8 hours or until set.

Spoon the custard over the jellies and top each glass with a dollop of
fromage frais. Decorate with the extra strawberries and lightly dust with
cocoa powder and icing sugar to serve.

*Raspberries are a delicious alternative to strawberries in this
trifle. Swap the jelly for a sugar-free raspberry variety too.*

rhubarb
and ginger crumble

serves 4

4 Syns per serving

✻ Ⓥ

ready in 45 minutes

500g rhubarb, trimmed
and cut into small pieces

3 tbsp sweetener

1 tsp ground ginger

finely grated zest
of ½ orange

fat free natural fromage
frais, sweetened to taste,
to serve

for the crumble

55g plain flour

35g extra-light spread

1 tsp ground ginger

1 tbsp sweetener

This amazing recipe brings together two very British passions: golden, crunchy crumble and tart, tender rhubarb. Go for 'forced' rhubarb if you can get it – this more delicate, watermelon-pink variety is grown under pots and is in season in the early months of the year.

Preheat your oven to 200°C/Fan 180°C/Gas 6.

Put the rhubarb, sweetener, ginger, orange zest and 5 tablespoons of water in a saucepan over a very low heat. Cover and simmer for 15 minutes until the flavours have combined. When the rhubarb is soft but still holding its shape, transfer it to a medium-sized baking dish.

To make the crumble, put the flour and spread in a bowl and rub together with your fingers until you have a soft, crumbly mixture. Mix in the ginger and sweetener with your fingers then scatter the topping over the rhubarb. Bake for 25 minutes or until golden and serve hot with a dollop of fat free fromage frais.

If you can't resist custard with your crumble, low fat cartons and cans are the lightest option at just ½ Syn per level tablespoon.

apple posset

Possets have been on the menu in Britain for hundreds of years, although originally they were served as sweetened drinks to cure colds! The modern version is a deliciously light pud with a hint of lemon that will really put a spring in your step.

serves 4

3½ Syns per serving

Ⓥ

ready in 45 minutes

4 large apples, peeled, cored and chopped, plus sliced apple to decorate

2 tbsp sweetener

1 tbsp lemon juice

2 large egg whites*

mint sprigs, to decorate

Pregnant women, the elderly and babies are advised not to eat raw or partially cooked eggs.

Put the apples in a saucepan with 150ml of water and a tablespoon of the sweetener. Bring to the boil over a high heat, reduce the heat to low and cook for 10 minutes or until tender.

Transfer the apples to a food processor and blend until smooth. Sieve the mixture into a bowl, stir in the lemon juice and set aside to cool.

Whisk the egg whites until soft peaks form then whisk in the remaining sweetener until the mixture is shiny and stiff.

Carefully fold the egg whites into the apple mixture until well combined then spoon into chilled dessert glasses or bowls. Chill for 2-3 hours and decorate with apple slices and mint sprigs to serve.

index

cook's tips

eggs

Pregnant women, the elderly and babies shouldn't eat raw or partially cooked eggs. We'll make a note in any recipes where raw or partially cooked eggs are used.

fat free natural fromage frais and yogurt

These are wonderful ingredients when you're Food Optimising as they give the creamy texture and taste normally achieved with cream. However, they tend to separate when boiled and can make the dish look unappetising. So unless the recipe says otherwise, add yogurt or fromage frais off the heat once all the other ingredients have been cooked and simply heat through. Both make great savoury or sweet ingredients – if you're using them to top a pudding, add sweetener and maybe some vanilla essence as well, to taste.

fresh, canned and frozen

Frozen ingredients and canned veg and beans are great alternatives to fresh foods and are so handy to keep in the cupboard or freezer. They'll keep for much longer, can be quicker to cook and are just as good for you. So feel free to switch between all three – bear in mind cooking times may change slightly.

fresh herbs

These lose their freshness quickly so if you have more than you can use, freeze them in a little water in ice cube trays – then you can add them straight to stews and curries.

fruit

While most fresh whole fruit is Free, puréed or cooked fruit counts as Syns because it isn't as filling and becomes much easier to over-consume. You'll see that in any recipes where fruit is puréed or cooked, we've counted it as Syns.

low calorie cooking spray

To cut down on fat in recipes, we recommend using non-stick cookware/bakeware wherever possible. However, where you do need to use fat then choose a low calorie cooking spray which contains 1 calorie or less per spray, as these are Free – others would need to be counted as Syns. Ideal for fried eggs, roast potatoes and chips!

meat and poultry

Trim off any visible fat before cooking to make lean meat or poultry Free, and remember to remove the skin before or after cooking poultry. If you cook poultry with the skin on, cook it separately from the other ingredients so that the fat can't run into them (eg don't roast potatoes in the same tin).

measurements

Syns for some ingredients are based on level teaspoons or tablespoons. Without measuring carefully, it's easy to far exceed your intended Syn intake without realising – so scrape a knife along the top of the spoon, knocking the excess back into the container. For best results, invest in a set of measuring spoons.

minced meat

Lean minced meat (5% fat or less) is a Free Food. Beef, pork and turkey mince are available in most major supermarkets at 5% fat or less – check the nutrition information to be sure. If possible, drain off any fat that comes from the mince while you're cooking it. No chicken and lamb mince is widely available with 5% fat or less so these would have a Syn value… unless you know a friendly butcher who'll mince skinless chicken breasts or lean lamb with all visible fat removed for you.

mustard powder

Made-up mustard in jars has Syns because it contains Synned ingredients while mustard powder is Free, making it a great choice for dressings and sauces.

seasoning

Where salt and pepper are used, we usually suggest seasoning to taste. Official advice is that adults should eat no more than 6g of salt a day – and bear in mind that small amounts can quickly add up.

stock

Fresh stock, stock cubes, stock pots, bouillon powder, ready-to-use liquid stock and liquid stock concentrate are all Free but be aware that gravy granules or powder and stock granules are not. Stock should normally be boiling when you add it to the pan, as cold stock will slow down cooking times.

symbol sense

ready in…

This gives a guide to how long the recipe will take to prepare and cook.

serves…

This gives you an idea of how many people the recipe can serve. However, feel free to split the recipe between more or fewer people instead, depending on how hungry you are – especially when it's Free!

freezer-friendly ✷

Recipes showing this symbol can be safely frozen for up to 1 month. Keep in mind official advice on freezing safely:

- Label food for the freezer with details of what the meal is and when you cooked it.

- Make sure food has cooled before you put it in the freezer.

- Defrost frozen meals completely and reheat thoroughly before eating.

Batch cooking: Wherever you see the freezer-friendly symbol ✷, you can save time and effort by cooking double or triple amounts and freezing the rest to enjoy at a later date. You'll usually save money too because it's often cheaper to buy ingredients in bulk.

suitable for vegetarians Ⓥ

Recipes marked with this symbol are suitable for vegetarians. Recipes that contain meat, fish or poultry can often be made vegetarian by using Quorn mince or pieces, textured vegetable protein/soya protein or tofu instead. Some ingredients that are unsuitable for vegetarians might surprise you – eg Parmesan, Worcestershire sauce, gelatine and Muller Light yogurts – although you can usually find a vegetarian alternative. It's always best to check the packaging to be sure.

First published in 2015 by
Slimming World
Clover Nook Road
Somercotes
Alfreton
Derbyshire
DE55 4SW
UK
www.slimmingworld.co.uk

Created and designed by
Slimming World's publications team
Publications manager: Allison Brentnall
Editor: Oliver Maxey
Designer: Kathryn Briggs

Recipes and food styling: Lorna Brash
Photography: Lara Holmes
Styling: Morag Farquhar

Front cover photograph: Cottage pie, page 12
Front cover photograph: Adrian Lawrence
Front cover food styling: Sunil Vijayakar

Back cover photographs, from top;
Honey-mustard roast beef with roasted roots, page 8
Jersey Royal potato salad, page 87
London particular soup, page 54
Rhubarb and ginger crumble, page 112

did you know?

10p from the sale of this book goes to our charitable foundation SMILES (Slimmers Making it a Little Easier for Someone), whose charity partners have included the NSPCC, Barnardo's, Cancer Research UK and the Marie Keating Foundation. In 2015 we donated almost £100,000 from book sales.